Introduction

Nothing is better than coming home to a nicely organized and clean home. Not only will you feel more relaxed in general but you'll simply enjoy your home more if you keep it organized. It's a lot easier than you may think initially to get organized, stay organized and make big time Spring Cleaning super easy to accomplish because it's mostly done already.

Let It Go

The common rule of whether to keep or toss something is if you haven't used it for an entire year, you're never going to use it. This is especially true of clothing because a year covers all the seasons.

Keep a donate container in your closet to put things in when you're in there. Each time the container is full, donate it to a thrift store or the Salvation Army. Keep a garbage bag for things that you can't donate.

Less is More

If you truly want an organized home one thing to keep in mind is that you don't need so much stuff. You can get by with one blush color and one little black dress.

What's more, if you buy less, you can buy higher quality merchandise that lasts longer, making it more of an investment than a whim purchase. Also, consider buying accessories to dress up or down an outfit over buying another outfit.

Use Clear Plastic Storage Boxes

To keep anything organized inside your closets clear plastic storage boxes and bags are the best things because you can see right through them. That way you don't have to dig up everything, causing a huge mess, to find your items. You'll just go into your closet and see right through the boxes or bags. If you can't afford to do that, use a label maker in the meantime.

A Zone a Day Keeps the Mess Away

If you organize your home into zones such as "coffee making zone", "makeup zone", "pet zone", "reading zone", and so forth you'll be able to identify one or two a day that you can clean up on a regular basis to avoid having to include every single part of your home in your Spring cleaning plans.

If you take just 15 to 20 minutes a day to clean up one of these zones extra well your house will soon always be company ready.

Stop Shopping for Things You Don't Need

Not only should you not go shopping for sport, you should stop shopping for things you don't need. Most of us, for example, have far too many clothes and wear the same ones, week after week anyway while all the new stuff collects dust.

If you are going to buy a new pair of jeans, for example, are you ready to toss the ones you're replacing? Always make a list and have a good reason for each purchase. If you plan your purchases in advance you'll not only keep your house more organized by bringing less stuff home, you'll also save money. Win-win!

Organize Your Home by Task

Zones were mentioned earlier and it's a good way to set up your home to keep things organized. Everyone likes doing things in certain ways. No way is right or wrong. Set up zones in your home by the way you live.

For example, if you like cutting your toenails in the living room and no one in the home objects, put your foot stuff near where you will use them in a pretty basket or closed container. That way you'll put it right back up when you're done.

Do Buy & Make Storage Solutions When Needed

For example, if you cook a lot, you likely have tons of spices that you cannot ever find. Get the type of spice rack you need to ensure that you can find what you want. Storage solutions can also be beautiful décor pieces if you think outside the box. A window seat with storage, an entertainment center with doors, a beautiful wrought iron coat rack are all great storage solutions that are also attractive.

If you have a lot of clothing you need to store during the seasons, lift your bed higher or buy one with drawers under it for added storage. Same with pots and pans or anything else you have. Don't just stack them in the bare cabinet, get the right storage solutions. Storage solutions are essential to an organized home. You'll be able to create a home for everything and keep it in its place easily with the right solutions.

Notice How You & Your Family Really Live

Notice that you drop your purse in the same general area, or you leave your hair dryer out in the same general place, or take your coat off and lay it someplace. Putting things away in such a way that they're hard to use is never going to work. You'll have to get strategic.

Does your spouse put his wallet on the kitchen table? Don't fight this. Add a beautiful handmade pottery bowl to the table to catch the wallet. Create storage solutions that keep in mind how you really live to make it easy and make things look organized.

Keep Travel Stuff in the Car

Other than food and perishables, the paraphernalia that you pack with you for your kids, and for you and your spouse to go on trips, can stay in the car. Make it a habit of replenishing diapers, socks, etc. that you used and then putting it back in the car as soon as possible.

This will also cut down on rushing around to pack in an emergency. You'll just need to grab a couple of items from the fridge, fill a couple bottles with water, and you're already on your way.

Use a Label Maker

No one wants labels to show up outside all their kitchen cabinets and closets around the house, this is not what I'm going to tell you to do. But, you can use labels inside cabinets and drawers to remind you and others what goes there. That way when you open the cabinet you'll see right on the inside of the door what goes there.

Labels can be especially helpful for children to learn to keep their property organized. If you label where your child's toys go, your child will have more fun cleaning up their messes because it won't feel overwhelming if each thing has a place to live.

Wicker Baskets Save The Day

Keep a wicker basket on each level of the house so that you can put things in there that go on the other level for easy distribution to its home. The basket won't look bad, in fact, you can buy beautiful wicker baskets of all colors in many stores like Target, Walmart, and if you're lucky enough to have one, Tuesday Morning.

Clean the Kitchen Immediately

Food should be put away within an hour or so anyway to avoid contamination and foodborne illness, so you may as well clean up the kitchen fully right after dinner. If you empty the dishwasher while you're cooking and load things in as you use them, it's simple because all you do is load the dishwasher and wipe down everything. Each person can put their own dish in the dishwasher.

Give Your Family Responsibility

One way to do this is to color code towels, dishes, and things each person uses. That way you know the pink cup in the living room belongs to Sue, and that blue towel in the bathroom floor belongs to Joe. They're going to be more likely to put things away if they know it can be traced to them. Another way is a chore list giving each family member rotating responsibility for various zones.

The Bathtub & Shower Trick That Hotels Use

One way to keep the bathtub and shower extra clean always is to train yourself and your family to use a towel, when they're done with their bath or shower, to wipe down and dry the walls and tub. Don't forget the shower curtain liner. This cuts down on soap scum, mold, and other grime without even having to use many cleaners.

Schedule Cleaning

The best way of all to keep your house clean so that Spring cleaning or cleaning for guests isn't a big deal is to keep a cleaning schedule. Set the times you should clean the carpet, deep clean the bathrooms, clean the fridge and more. Just like you have to change your AC filter periodically you should be deep cleaning some things in your home monthly and some yearly.

You can have a more organized home and be "Spring Cleaning" ready at the drop of a hat if you think ahead. Once you get your house set up properly you will realize that you spend less time on housework than you did before you got organized.

Room checklists

Room _____

Weekly	Monthly
☐ _____	☐ _____
☐ _____	☐ _____
☐ _____	☐ _____
☐ _____	☐ _____
☐ _____	☐ _____
☐ _____	☐ _____
☐ _____	☐ _____
☐ _____	☐ _____
☐ _____	☐ _____
☐ _____	☐ _____
☐ _____	☐ _____
☐ _____	☐ _____
☐ _____	☐ _____
☐ _____	☐ _____

Quarterly	Semi Annual
☐ _____	☐ _____
☐ _____	☐ _____
☐ _____	☐ _____

Annual

☐ _____

Notes

Room _____

Weekly

- [ ] _____
- [ ] _____
- [ ] _____
- [ ] _____
- [ ] _____
- [ ] _____
- [ ] _____
- [ ] _____
- [ ] _____
- [ ] _____
- [ ] _____
- [ ] _____
- [ ] _____

Monthly

_____
_____
_____
_____
_____
_____
_____
_____
_____
_____
_____
_____
_____

Quarterly

- [ ] _____
- [ ] _____
- [ ] _____

Semi Annual

- [ ] _____
- [ ] _____
- [ ] _____

Annual

- [ ] _____
- [ ] _____

Notes

Room _____

Weekly

- [ ] _____
- [ ] _____
- [ ] _____
- [ ] _____
- [ ] _____
- [ ] _____
- [ ] _____
- [ ] _____
- [ ] _____
- [ ] _____
- [ ] _____
- [ ] _____

Monthly

_____
_____
_____
_____
_____
_____
_____
_____
_____
_____
_____
_____

Quarterly

- [ ] _____
- [ ] _____
- [ ] _____

Semi Annual

- [ ] _____
- [ ] _____
- [ ] _____

Annual

- [ ] _____

- [ ] _____

Notes

Room _____

Weekly	Monthly
☐ _____	_____
☐ _____	_____
☐ _____	_____
☐ _____	_____
☐ _____	_____
☐ _____	_____
☐ _____	_____
☐ _____	_____
☐ _____	_____
☐ _____	_____
☐ _____	_____
☐ _____	_____
☐ _____	_____

Quarterly	Semi Annual
☐ _____	☐ _____
☐ _____	☐ _____
☐ _____	☐ _____

Annual	
☐ _____	☐ _____

Notes

Room _____

Weekly

☐ _____
☐ _____
☐ _____
☐ _____
☐ _____
☐ _____
☐ _____
☐ _____
☐ _____
☐ _____
☐ _____
☐ _____

Monthly

_____
_____
_____
_____
_____
_____
_____
_____
_____
_____
_____
_____

Quarterly

☐ _____
☐ _____
☐ _____

Semi Annual

☐ _____
☐ _____
☐ _____

Annual

☐ _____

☐ _____

Notes

Room _____

Weekly

- [ ] _____
- [ ] _____
- [ ] _____
- [ ] _____
- [ ] _____
- [ ] _____
- [ ] _____
- [ ] _____
- [ ] _____
- [ ] _____
- [ ] _____
- [ ] _____
- [ ] _____

Monthly

- _____
- _____
- _____
- _____
- _____
- _____
- _____
- _____
- _____
- _____
- _____
- _____
- _____

Quarterly

- [ ] _____
- [ ] _____
- [ ] _____

Semi Annual

- [ ] _____
- [ ] _____
- [ ] _____

Annual

- [ ] _____

- [ ] _____

Notes

Room _____

Weekly	Monthly
☐ _____	_____
☐ _____	_____
☐ _____	_____
☐ _____	_____
☐ _____	_____
☐ _____	_____
☐ _____	_____
☐ _____	_____
☐ _____	_____
☐ _____	_____
☐ _____	_____
☐ _____	_____

Quarterly	Semi Annual
☐ _____	☐ _____
☐ _____	☐ _____
☐ _____	☐ _____

Annual	
☐ _____	☐ _____

Notes

Room _____

Weekly	Monthly

☐ _____
☐ _____
☐ _____
☐ _____
☐ _____
☐ _____
☐ _____
☐ _____
☐ _____
☐ _____
☐ _____
☐ _____
☐ _____

_____
_____
_____
_____
_____
_____
_____
_____
_____
_____
_____
_____
_____

Quarterly	Semi Annual

☐ _____
☐ _____
☐ _____

☐ _____
☐ _____
☐ _____

Annual	

☐ _____   ☐ _____

Notes

Room _____

Weekly	Monthly
☐ _____	_____
☐ _____	_____
☐ _____	_____
☐ _____	_____
☐ _____	_____
☐ _____	_____
☐ _____	_____
☐ _____	_____
☐ _____	_____
☐ _____	_____
☐ _____	_____
☐ _____	_____
☐ _____	_____

Quarterly	Semi Annual
☐ _____	☐ _____
☐ _____	☐ _____
☐ _____	☐ _____

Annual	
☐ _____	☐ _____

Notes

Room _____

Weekly	Monthly

☐ _____
☐ _____
☐ _____
☐ _____
☐ _____
☐ _____
☐ _____
☐ _____
☐ _____
☐ _____
☐ _____
☐ _____
☐ _____

Quarterly	Semi Annual

☐ _____
☐ _____
☐ _____

Annual

☐ _____

Notes

Notes

Weekly Schedules

Cleaning Checklist

Week ending _____

	M	T	W	T	F	S	S
_____							
_____							
_____							
_____							
_____							
_____							
_____							
_____							
_____							
_____							

Notes

Cleaning Checklist

Week ending _____

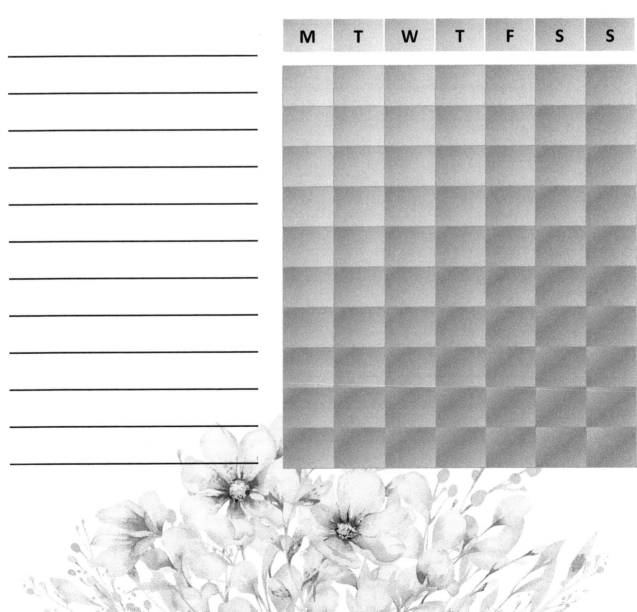

M	T	W	T	F	S	S

Notes

Cleaning Checklist

Week ending _____

	M	T	W	T	F	S	S
_____							
_____							
_____							
_____							
_____							
_____							
_____							
_____							
_____							
_____							
_____							

Notes

Cleaning Checklist

Week ending _____

_____

_____

_____

_____

_____

_____

_____

_____

_____

_____

M	T	W	T	F	S	S

Notes

_____
_____
_____
_____
_____
_____
_____
_____
_____
_____
_____
_____
_____
_____
_____

Cleaning Checklist

Week ending _____

M	T	W	T	F	S	S

Notes

Cleaning Checklist

Week ending _____

M	T	W	T	F	S	S

Notes

Cleaning Checklist

Week ending _____

M	T	W	T	F	S	S

Notes

Cleaning Checklist

Week ending _____

	M	T	W	T	F	S	S
_____							
_____							
_____							
_____							
_____							
_____							
_____							
_____							
_____							
_____							

Notes

Cleaning Checklist

Week ending _____

	M	T	W	T	F	S	S
_____							
_____							
_____							
_____							
_____							
_____							
_____							
_____							
_____							
_____							

Notes

Cleaning Checklist

Week ending _____

	M	T	W	T	F	S	S
_____							
_____							
_____							
_____							
_____							
_____							
_____							
_____							
_____							
_____							

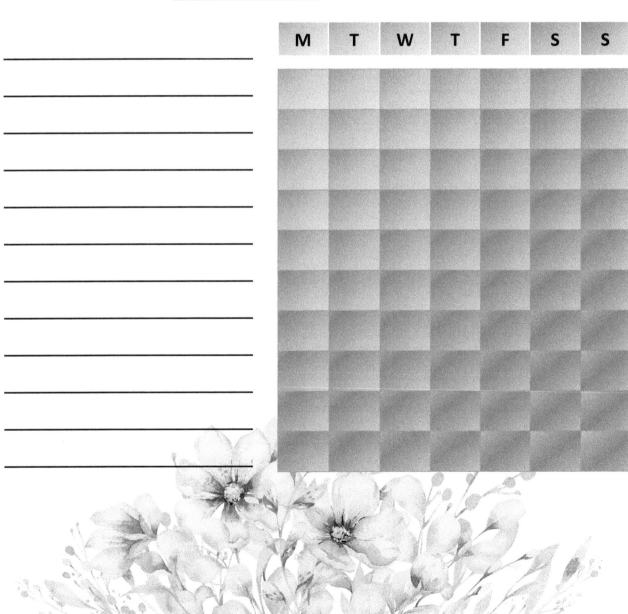

Notes

Cleaning Checklist

Week ending _____

	M	T	W	T	F	S	S
_____							
_____							
_____							
_____							
_____							
_____							
_____							
_____							
_____							
_____							

Notes

Cleaning Checklist

Week ending _____

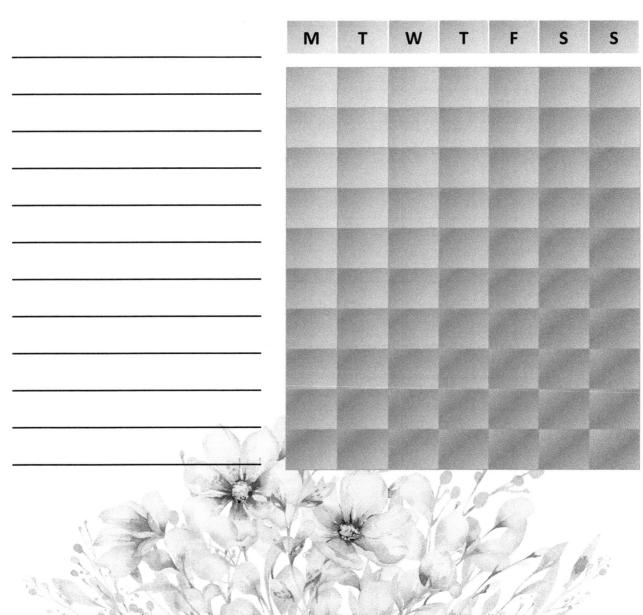

	M	T	W	T	F	S	S
_____							
_____							
_____							
_____							
_____							
_____							
_____							
_____							
_____							
_____							
_____							

Notes

Cleaning Checklist

Week ending _____

M	T	W	T	F	S	S

Notes

Cleaning Checklist

Week ending _____

M	T	W	T	F	S	S

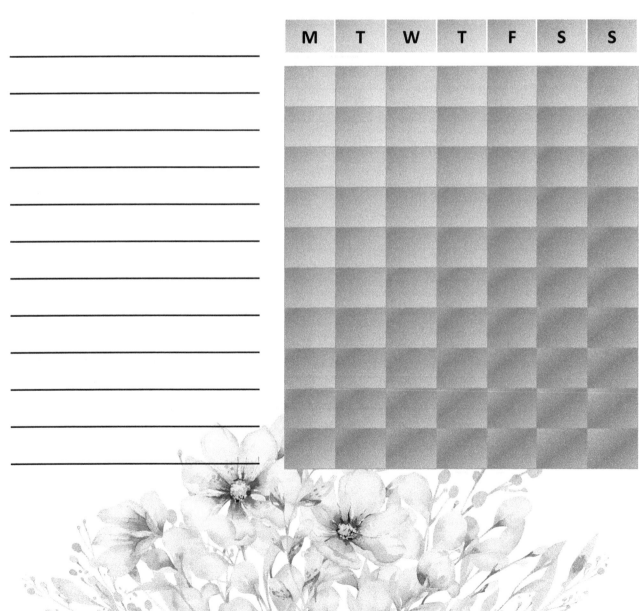

Notes

Cleaning Checklist

Week ending _____

	M	T	W	T	F	S	S
_____							
_____							
_____							
_____							
_____							
_____							
_____							
_____							
_____							
_____							

Notes

Cleaning Checklist

Week ending _____

	M	T	W	T	F	S	S
_____							
_____							
_____							
_____							
_____							
_____							
_____							
_____							
_____							
_____							

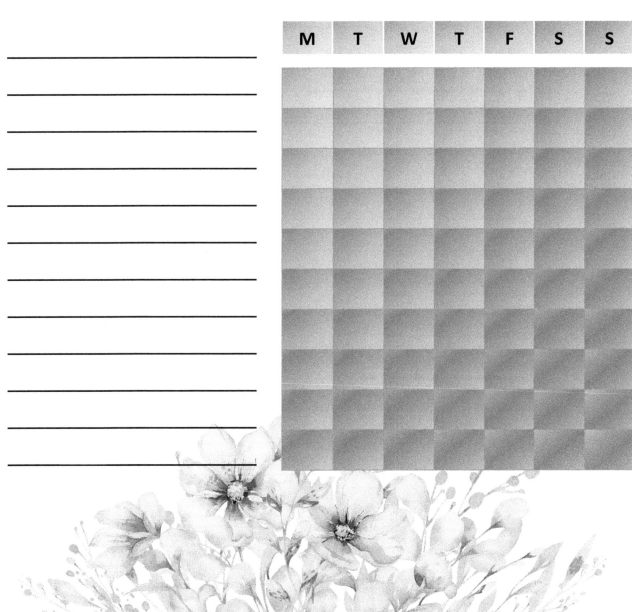

Notes

_____
_____
_____
_____
_____
_____
_____
_____
_____
_____
_____
_____
_____
_____
_____
_____

Cleaning Checklist

Week ending _____

	M	T	W	T	F	S	S
_____							
_____							
_____							
_____							
_____							
_____							
_____							
_____							
_____							
_____							
_____							

Notes

Cleaning Checklist

Week ending _____

	M	T	W	T	F	S	S
_____							
_____							
_____							
_____							
_____							
_____							
_____							
_____							
_____							
_____							

Notes

Cleaning Checklist

Week ending _____

	M	T	W	T	F	S	S
_____							
_____							
_____							
_____							
_____							
_____							
_____							
_____							
_____							
_____							

Notes

Cleaning Checklist

Week ending _____

M	T	W	T	F	S	S

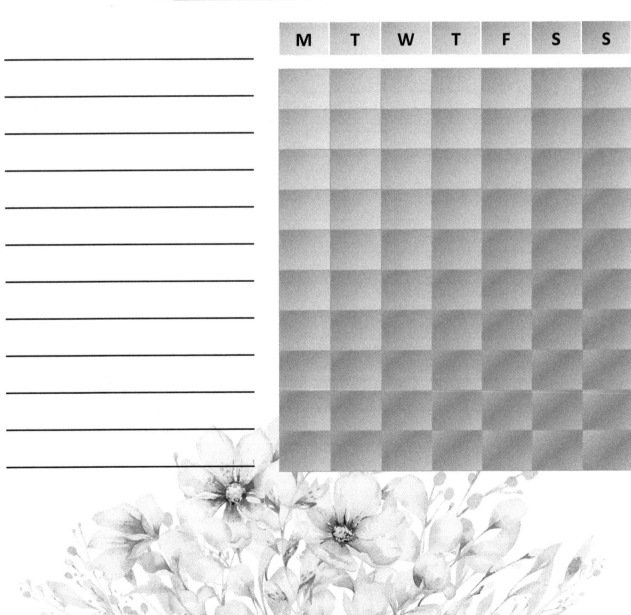

Notes

Cleaning Checklist

Week ending _____

M	T	W	T	F	S	S

Notes

Cleaning Checklist

Week ending _____

M	T	W	T	F	S	S

Notes

Cleaning Checklist

Week ending _____

	M	T	W	T	F	S	S
_____							
_____							
_____							
_____							
_____							
_____							
_____							
_____							
_____							
_____							

Notes

Cleaning Checklist

Week ending _____

_____
_____
_____
_____
_____
_____
_____
_____
_____
_____

M	T	W	T	F	S	S

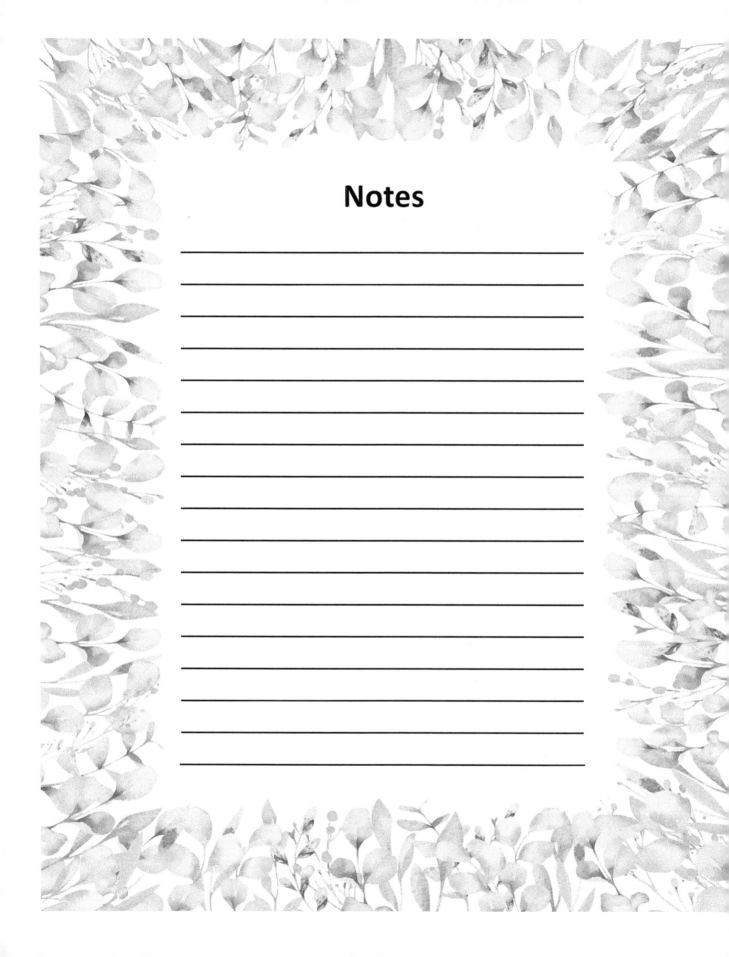
Notes

Cleaning Checklist

Week ending _____

	M	T	W	T	F	S	S
_____							
_____							
_____							
_____							
_____							
_____							
_____							
_____							
_____							
_____							

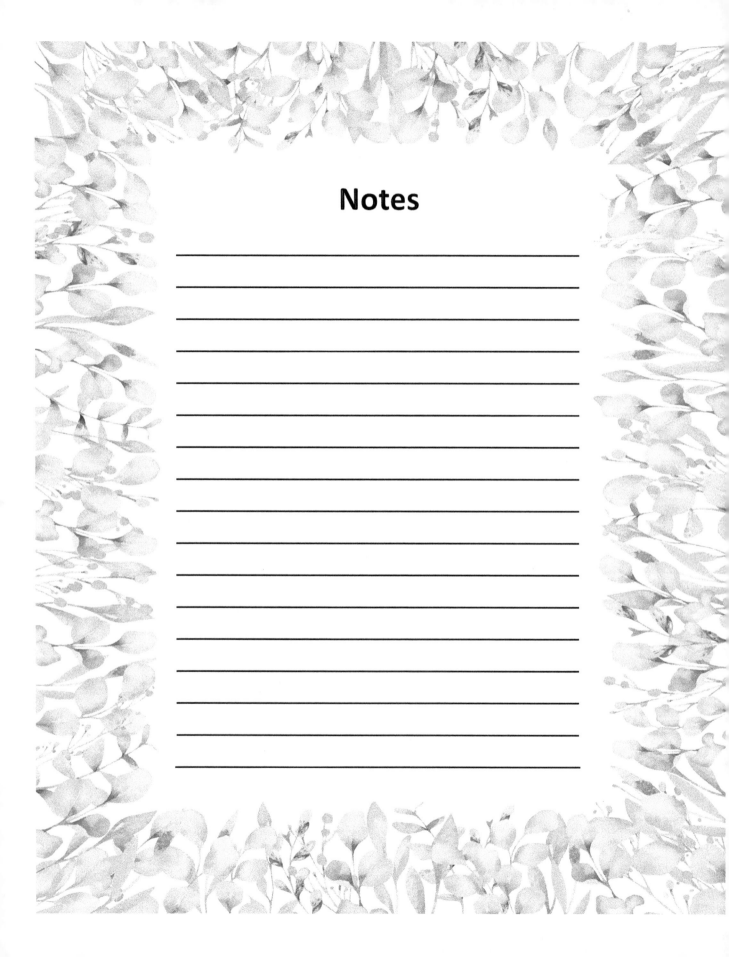

Cleaning Checklist

Week ending _____

	M	T	W	T	F	S	S
_____							
_____							
_____							
_____							
_____							
_____							
_____							
_____							
_____							
_____							

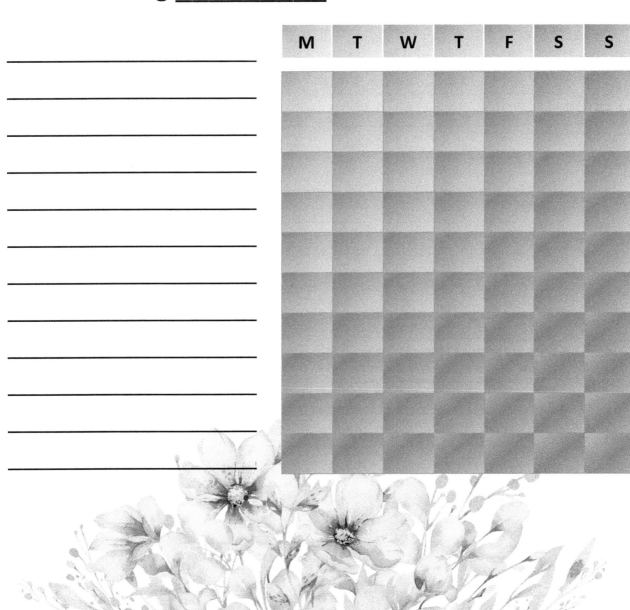

Notes

Cleaning Checklist

Week ending _____

M	T	W	T	F	S	S

Notes

Cleaning Checklist

Week ending _____

	M	T	W	T	F	S	S
_____							
_____							
_____							
_____							
_____							
_____							
_____							
_____							
_____							
_____							

Notes

Cleaning Checklist

Week ending _____

	M	T	W	T	F	S	S
_____							
_____							
_____							
_____							
_____							
_____							
_____							
_____							
_____							
_____							
_____							

Notes

Cleaning Checklist

Week ending _____

	M	T	W	T	F	S	S
_____							
_____							
_____							
_____							
_____							
_____							
_____							
_____							
_____							
_____							
_____							

Notes

_____
_____
_____
_____
_____
_____
_____
_____
_____
_____
_____
_____
_____
_____
_____
_____

Cleaning Checklist

Week ending _____

	M	T	W	T	F	S	S
_____							
_____							
_____							
_____							
_____							
_____							
_____							
_____							
_____							
_____							

Notes

Cleaning Checklist

Week ending _____

M	T	W	T	F	S	S

Notes

_____
_____
_____
_____
_____
_____
_____
_____
_____
_____
_____
_____
_____
_____
_____

Cleaning Checklist

Week ending _____

	M	T	W	T	F	S	S
_____							
_____							
_____							
_____							
_____							
_____							
_____							
_____							
_____							
_____							

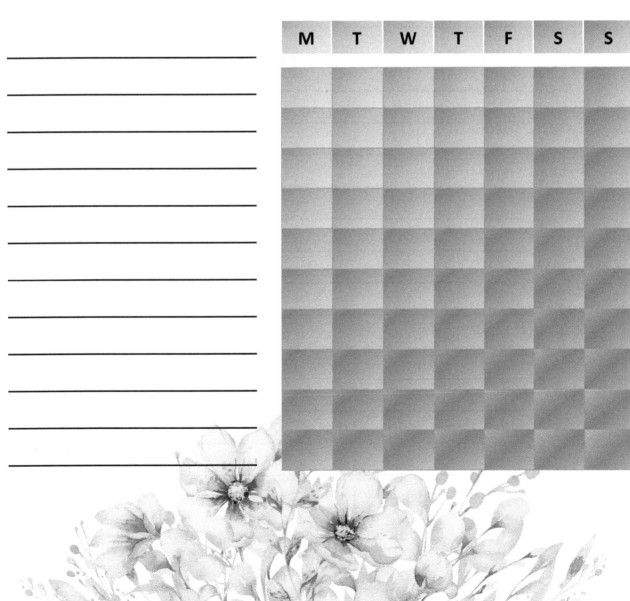

Notes

Cleaning Checklist

Week ending _____

	M	T	W	T	F	S	S
_____							
_____							
_____							
_____							
_____							
_____							
_____							
_____							
_____							
_____							

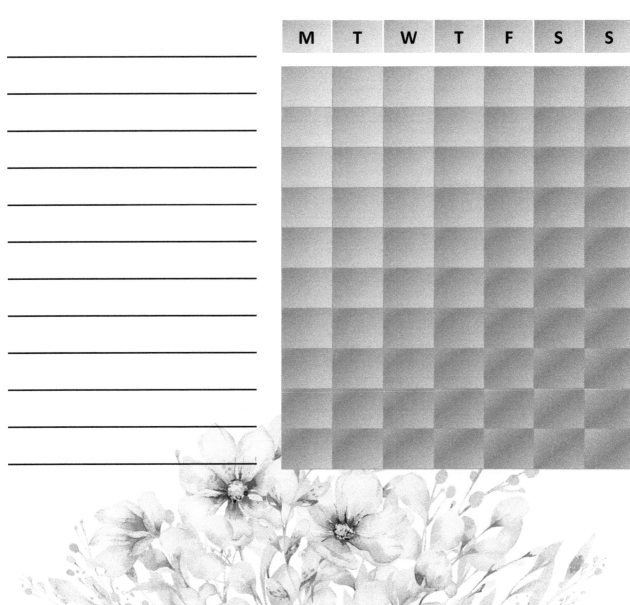

Notes

Cleaning Checklist

Week ending _____

	M	T	W	T	F	S	S
_____							
_____							
_____							
_____							
_____							
_____							
_____							
_____							
_____							
_____							

Notes

Cleaning Checklist

Week ending _____

	M	T	W	T	F	S	S
_____							
_____							
_____							
_____							
_____							
_____							
_____							
_____							
_____							
_____							

Notes

Cleaning Checklist

Week ending _____

	M	T	W	T	F	S	S
_____							
_____							
_____							
_____							
_____							
_____							
_____							
_____							
_____							
_____							

Notes

Cleaning Checklist

Week ending _____

	M	T	W	T	F	S	S
_____							
_____							
_____							
_____							
_____							
_____							
_____							
_____							
_____							
_____							
_____							

Notes

Cleaning Checklist

Week ending _____

M	T	W	T	F	S	S

Notes

Cleaning Checklist

Week ending _____

M	T	W	T	F	S	S

Notes

Cleaning Checklist

Week ending _____

	M	T	W	T	F	S	S
_____							
_____							
_____							
_____							
_____							
_____							
_____							
_____							
_____							
_____							

Notes

Cleaning Checklist

Week ending _____

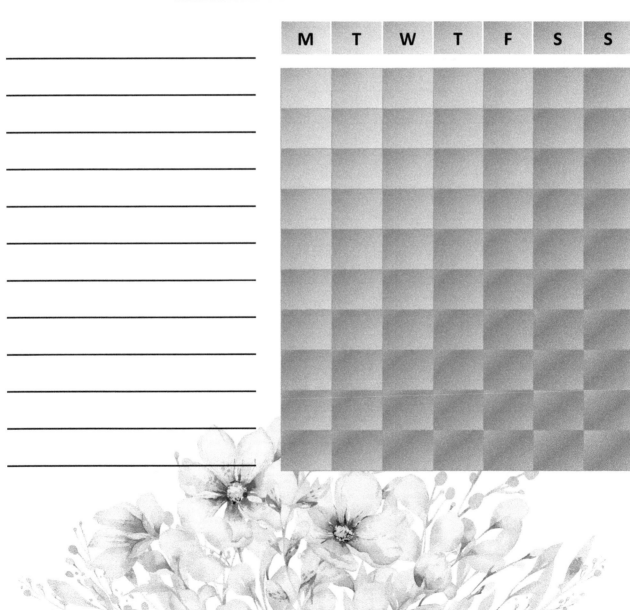

M	T	W	T	F	S	S

Notes

Cleaning Checklist

Week ending _____

_____
_____
_____
_____
_____
_____
_____
_____
_____
_____
_____

M	T	W	T	F	S	S

Notes

Cleaning Checklist

Week ending _____

M	T	W	T	F	S	S

Notes

Cleaning Checklist

Week ending _____

M	T	W	T	F	S	S

Notes

Cleaning Checklist

Week ending _____

	M	T	W	T	F	S	S
_____							
_____							
_____							
_____							
_____							
_____							
_____							
_____							
_____							
_____							
_____							

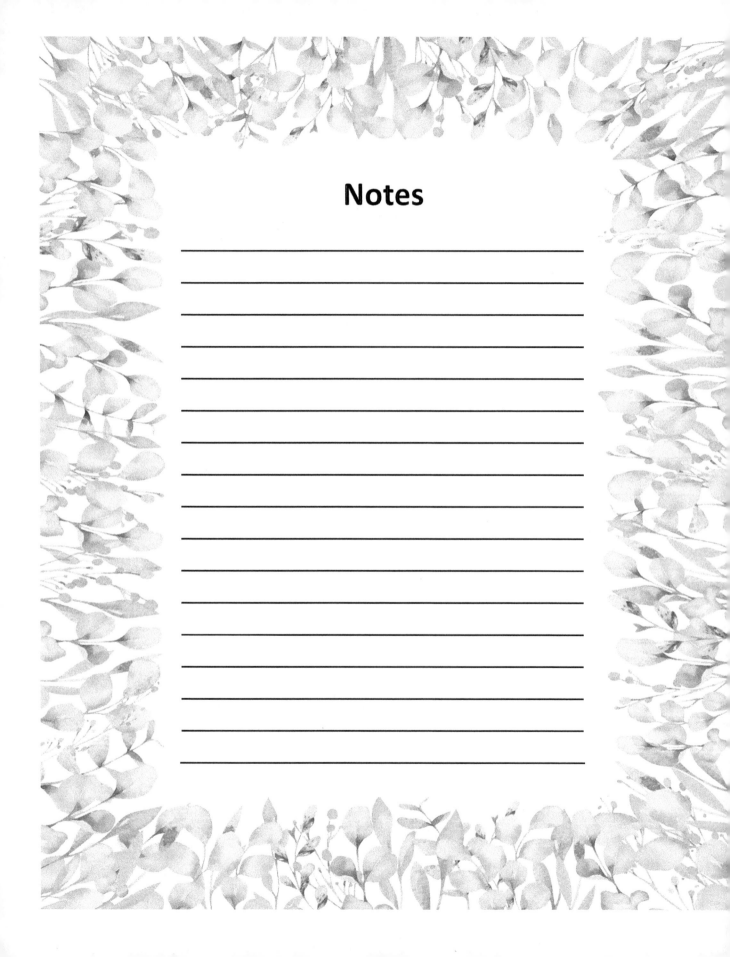

Cleaning Checklist

Week ending _____

	M	T	W	T	F	S	S
_____							
_____							
_____							
_____							
_____							
_____							
_____							
_____							
_____							
_____							

Cleaning Checklist

Week ending _____

	M	T	W	T	F	S	S
_____							
_____							
_____							
_____							
_____							
_____							
_____							
_____							
_____							
_____							

Notes

Cleaning Checklist

Week ending _____

	M	T	W	T	F	S	S
_____							
_____							
_____							
_____							
_____							
_____							
_____							
_____							
_____							
_____							
_____							

Notes

Cleaning Checklist

Week ending _____

M	T	W	T	F	S	S

Notes

Cleaning Checklist

Week ending _____

	M	T	W	T	F	S	S
_____							
_____							
_____							
_____							
_____							
_____							
_____							
_____							
_____							
_____							
_____							

Notes

CPSIA information can be obtained
at www.ICGtesting.com
Printed in the USA
LVHW020131090121
675855LV00008B/360